POSITIVE SPORTS PARENTING

How "Second-Goal" Parents Raise Winners in Life Through Sports

By Jim Thompson

BALANCE SPORTS
PUBLISHING

Balance Sports Publishing, LLC · Portola Valley, California

Balance Sports Publishing, LLC
195 Lucero Way
Portola Valley, CA 94028
(650) 391-9850

LIBRARY OF CONGRESS CATALOG-IN-PRINTING DATA
Thompson, Jim, 1949-
    Positive sports parenting : how "second-goal" parents raise winners in life through sports / by Jim Thompson. — 1st ed.

        p. ; cm.

    ISBN: 978-0-9821317-1-8

1. Sports for children—Psychological aspects. 2. Parent and child. I. Title.

GV709.2 .T5 2009
796/.083

FIRST EDITION
Printed in the United States of America

10 9 8   19 18

Designed by Elisa Tanaka

Table of Contents

Table of Contents *continued*

Preface

Before I started Positive Coaching Alliance, before I was a coach, I was a sports parent.

My son started playing sports as I enrolled in the Stanford University Graduate School of Business in 1984. The first year of business school was incredibly challenging for me, so I had no fantasies of coaching my son's first seasons of soccer, basketball, and T-ball.

Each Saturday I would leave the library long enough to watch Gabriel's games and ask the questions sports parents ask. Was my son doing okay? Did he have potential to play in high school, in college, beyond? Was he being treated fairly by his coaches, teammates, the opposing teams, and officials?

And, if I am truthful about it, I wondered at some deep level: Was he making me look good (or bad) as a parent?

These original hopes and fears of a typical sports parent were the seeds of Positive Coaching Alliance (PCA), a movement I started at the Stanford Department of Athletics in 1998. Since then, PCA has partnered with more than a thousand youth sports organizations and high schools, serving three million youth athletes across the country, in pursuit of our mission: *to transform youth sports so sports can transform youth.*

PCA's goal is to change the culture of youth sports so every

- Coach is a **Double-Goal Coach®** who prepares athletes to win and teaches life lessons through sports

- Athlete aspires to be a **Triple-Impact Competitor®** who makes self, teammates, and the game better

- Sports parent becomes a **Second-Goal Parent**® who concentrates on his/her child's character development while letting athletes and coaches focus on the first goal of winning on the scoreboard

This vision is shared by a growing number of prominent coaches, athletes, and youth sports experts who comprise PCA's National Advisory Board, including:

Dusty Baker, Former MLB Player & Manager

Shane Battier, Retired Two-Time NBA Champion Player and Past NCAA Basketball Player of the Year

Ruthie Bolton, Olympic Basketball Gold Medalist and Former WNBA Player

Brandi Chastain, World Cup Soccer Champion, Olympic Gold Medalist

Joe Ehrman, Former NFL Pro Bowl Player and Founder, Coach For America

Julie Foudy, World Cup Soccer Champion, Olympic Gold Medalist

Peter Haberl, USOC Senior Sport Psychologist

Phil Jackson, 11-Time NBA Champion Coach

Tony La Russa, Three-Time World Series Champion Former Major League Baseball Manager

Mark Murphy, CEO, Green Bay Packers

Doc Rivers, NBA Champion Head Coach

Summer Sanders, Olympic Swimming Gold Medalist

Steve Young, Pro Football Hall of Famer and San Francisco 49ers Super Bowl Champion Quarterback

The ideas and practical tools in this book – gleaned from more than a decade's experience working with youth sports organizations and from conversations with experts and thousands of sports parents – are designed to help parents help their children get the most from their sports experience. You have a crucially important role to play to help your child become the best person he or she can be. You and your child deserve the very best.

Jim Thompson
Founder and Executive Director, Positive Coaching Alliance
www.PositiveCoach.org

1

The Second-Goal Parent: A Focus on the Big Picture

I have long been a fan of "The Family Circus" comic strip. Perhaps my favorite strip of all time features the family dog barking up a storm in the middle of the night. Dad, irritated that he's been awakened from a much-needed sleep, clomps down the stairs to yell at Barfy, who dutifully hangs his head. Dad climbs back up the stairs while the cartoonist has a surprise for us. He pans back so we see in the far corner of the yard a burglar retreating.

We who see the "Big Picture" know Barfy has protected his family from a burglary. The dad, seeing only the "Little Picture," is angry at being disturbed.

This comic strip can serve as a metaphor for youth sports. Youth coaches and parents are often overwhelmed by so many Little Pictures filled with barking dogs that they miss the Big Picture entirely. How our children do in a sporting event is Little Picture. Whether they win or lose, play well or badly, laugh or whine after the game – all Little Picture.

What children take away from youth sports to help them become successful, contributing members of society is the Big Picture. Whether they remain physically active throughout life, learn to bounce back from difficulties with renewed determination, discover how to support other people within a team context – these are the Big Picture.

The Big Picture and You

This book describes a model of sports parenting that focuses relentlessly on the Big Picture. We call it the Second-Goal Parent.

There are two broad goals in youth sports: striving to win and building character so kids develop into successful, contributing members of society.

As important as winning is, Second-Goal Parents let coaches and athletes worry about the first goal of scoreboard results. *Second-Goal Parents have a much more important role to play: ensuring their children take away from sports lessons that will help them be successful in life.* Remember, that is the Big Picture. And attending to this is much more vital than being an extraneous back-seat coach.

Now, there is nothing wrong with caring about whether your child's team wins or loses. Go ahead and care about it! Likewise, there's nothing wrong with playing catch or shooting baskets or enjoying playing any sport with your child – or even giving pointers when your child asks for them.

But the lifelong impact you can have – that no one else can in quite the way you can – is on the life lessons your child takes away from the sports experience. No one can be there for your child in this way better than you. No one.

If you embrace your role as a Second-Goal Parent, it will transform the way you see youth sports. It will help you act to seize the teachable moments that will come your way again and again because you are looking for them.

What might have seemed like a disappointing loss or a failure by your child becomes an opportunity to reinforce resiliency. A tough competition in forbiddingly hot, cold, or nasty weather can prompt a conversation with your child about learning to enjoy challenges. Whether your child succeeds or fails on the playing field, you will be able to use the experiences to reinforce the kind of person you want him to be.

Honing a Second-Goal Focus

Let's say your child has just had an opportunity to make the winning play in a game and blew it. If you played the sport (and perhaps even if you didn't), you may have suggestions for how the child could have made the play. We call this a "First-Goal focus" because it concentrates on helping your child do well on the scoreboard, which the larger sports culture always puts first.

My two decades of experience working with sports parents has taught me that First-Goal suggestions from parents are often not well received by their child. Athletes get so much coaching already – from coaches, from teammates, from the game itself. When parents add to this flood of coaching, it often overwhelms the child, like the proverbial straw that breaks the camel's back.

Instead of being a back-seat coach, hone a Second-Goal focus with your child. Rather than obsessing about the skills and strategy of the game, engage your child around the life lessons from their experience.

For example, on the car ride home after a game, focus on the second goal. Use questions and your own assertions (sparingly).

Questions

- "What did you learn from that experience?"

- "Why do you think it's important to learn to bounce back from failure?"

- "What about the game can you feel good about even though you lost?"

Assertions

- "I know in my life that I learn more from my failures than from my successes. In fact, times I've been successful have usually come from learning from my mistakes."

- "I'm proud of the way you dealt with the pressure during the game. Many people get so afraid under pressure that they don't give their best effort. You didn't make the play, but you gave it a good shot!"

- "Resilience is such an important attribute. I love to see you bounce back after a disappointment."

Back to the Big Picture

The signature act of a Second-Goal Parent is relentlessly keeping one's eye on the Big Picture. Second-Goal Parents hear the barking dogs but don't allow themselves to get distracted from their goal of ensuring their children get the most from their youth sports experience. They develop a "muscle" that allows them to focus on the Big Picture even when others are freaking out over a First-Goal issue like an official's bad call.

I know from personal experience how hard this is. My hope for this book is that it will inspire and help you become a Second-Goal Parent with an eye on the Big Picture so your child can have the very best sports experience possible.

Chapter 1 Take-Aways

1 Adults in youth sports too often get caught up in the Little Picture (performance on the field) and lose sight of the Big Picture (life lessons learned on the field).

2 There are two broad goals in youth sports: striving to win and building character so that kids develop into productive, contributing members of society.

3 Second-Goal Parents let coaches and athletes worry about winning. Parents have a much more important role: focusing on teachable moments and the life lessons that their children can take away from sports.

CHAPTER TWO

First Things First: Getting Straight with Goals

"My dad coached all of my youth soccer teams while I was growing up, and we were always fighting over what had happened during the game that day, or how I wasn't working hard enough in practice...Then my dad took the Positive Coaching Alliance classes. Since then, he has definitely eased up, and it is much easier for both of us to take advice from each other and understand where the other person is coming from. Since PCA, my dad and I get along so much better, on and off the field."

Christina, Youth Soccer Player

In the course of speaking to thousands of sports parents all across the United States, I've noticed the sharp tension that often exists between parent and athlete. What should be a wonderful shared experience too often becomes a source of conflict between parent and child. Christina's experience above is far from unusual.

This is too bad because a family's experience with youth sports has the potential to enhance the relationship between parent and child for a lifetime – long after the days on the playing field have ended.

The place where parent-athlete relationships usually start to go wrong is with goals. Parents often don't take the time to explicitly examine their own goals for their child in sports or ensure that their behavior is consistent with their identified goals.

Nor do they consider that their goals may not match their child's goals.

The 100-Points Exercise

We start PCA parent workshops with an exercise that gets right to the heart of this issue. I encourage you to take the time to fill out this form right now. I am confident you won't be sorry.

You have 100 "points" that you can divide across the goals on the form (or a separate piece of paper) in any way you want. You can even write in your own goals if the form doesn't have all the ones that are important to you. Remember to fill out the form in terms of what your goals for your child in sports are (later we'll address your child's goals). Your points should add up to 100, more or less – no one's watching!

What are YOUR goals for your child in youth sports?
_____ Become a good athlete
_____ Learn to play the sport
_____ Learn teamwork
_____ Win
_____ Gain increased self-confidence
_____ Learn to deal with defeat
_____ Physical fitness
_____ Learn "life lessons"
_____ Have fun
_____ Make friends
_____ Earn a college scholarship
_____ Other (specify: _____)
_____ Other (specify: _____)
_____ Other (specify: _____)
100 TOTAL

What Parents Say

In hundreds of workshops, we have learned that most parents have similar hopes and goals for their athletes: physical fitness, having fun, making friends, increased self-confidence, and learning life lessons.

A father once gave all 100 points to having fun because he said that all the other benefits become possible if his child sticks with sports. And if he is having fun, he'll keep coming back. If it stops being fun, he won't continue and the many benefits listed here will be lost.

Many parents resonate with the goal of learning to deal with defeat without becoming defeated. I've heard moving testimonials about parents rebounding from failure in their jobs to ultimately experience success. People nod their heads when I note that it's hard to learn how to bounce back from defeat if you don't experience defeat.

Rarely do parents give many points to winning. In the low-key atmosphere of a classroom or cafeteria, winning doesn't get much respect.

How Parents Act

Then comes the moment of revelation. We say to the parents, "You've given most of your points to these wonderful benefits of youth sports. But what happens when you go to a youth sports competition? All but one of these items goes out the window. Which one seems to get all 100 points if we look at the way parents act on the sidelines?"

This leads to sheepish expressions because we all have acted in conflict with our goals and made *winning* the be-all and end-all of youth sports.

Your 100 Points

Let's look at your 100 points. Are there any surprises? Any areas where you need to bring your sideline behavior in line with your goals?

Your Child's 100 Points

If your child is older than 7 or 8, sit down with her and ask her to fill out this form. (See page 56.) This may produce some "aha moments" with big disconnects between your goals and hers. When asked, most kids say they play sports for fun, to make friends, and to learn to play the sport.

This can lead to a wonderful discussion. Ask why she distributed her points the way she did. Don't say much at this point – get her talking about *her* goals. Ask open-ended questions such as, "You have 50 points on 'Fun.' Why so many points on that?" Then really listen.

You can extend the conversation by comparing how many points you gave to a specific item with how many your daughter did.

Putting Your Goals into Action

Here are two tools to make practical use of the 100-Points Exercise.

Targeted Cheering

Targeted Cheering helps you avoid getting sucked into the win-at-all-cost mentality that throws the other goals of youth sports out the window. Let's go back to your 100-Point form.

1) Put a star by the three to five top goals you identified.

2) Write a "cheer" for each goal. For example, to reinforce the importance of effort, teamwork, or resilience, target your cheering to that particular quality regardless of whether the action on the field results in a score.

"Great effort, Sam! Way to work hard!"

"Way to help out on defense, Carmen. Nice teamwork!"

"That's a tough break, Lexi. Go get 'em next time!"

3) Put your sheet of cheers in your billfold or purse and bring it to your child's games. Use it to focus your cheering on the goals you identified as most important to you.

4) During the car ride home, reinforce your goals. "Chris, I liked how you bounced up after you fell on that breakaway. That's determination!"

No-Directions Cheering

It's disconcerting for athletes to have parents yell out instructions.

Avoid giving your child advice on the sidelines by committing to No-Directions Cheering. Eliminate verbs in your cheering because you can't give advice without verbs. For example, "Pass the ball to Sarah" is a no-no because it uses the word "pass" as a verb to give directions. On the other hand, "Great pass, Sarah!" gives no directions. You're just commenting (appreciatively) on what you see Sarah doing.

Here are some examples of No-Directions Cheering:

- "Great effort!"
- "Good hustle!"
- "Way to play defense!"
- "Nice hit!"
- "Terrific play!"
- "Way to go!"

No-Directions Cheering is important because your child will do better if it's his game. So provide encouragement without direction – or even enjoy the game in silence. The more space you leave him to be the actor – a proactive player rather than a puppet on your string – the better.

Chapter 2 Take-Aways

1 Make sure you are clear on your goals for your child in sports. Use the 100-Point Exercise to help clarify them.

2 Let your child do the 100-Point Exercise, and then have a discussion about your respective goals. Listen more than talk.

3 During games, use Targeted Cheering and No-Directions Cheering to make sure your actions on the sidelines are consistent with your goals.

CHAPTER THREE

Transforming the Culture of Youth Sports

Professional sports is a business whose goal is making a profit by entertaining fans. That usually requires a winning team, which leads to a win-at-all-cost mentality. Unfortunately, professional sports and the media surrounding it have become powerful to the point that youth sports too often mimics professional sports.

Because the playing surfaces, rules, and equipment are similar for professional and youth sports, people tend to confuse them. But they are fundamentally different enterprises. Youth sports is about using sports to develop great people – that's the Big Picture! The scoreboard is a powerful tool for helping that happen, not an end in itself.

Unfortunately, many adults have lost sight of the Big Picture of youth sports and instead default to the win-at-all-cost mentality prevalent in professional sports. Go to virtually any youth sports event and you'll see adults – coaches and parents – stomping, yelling, and even fighting about Little Picture issues like playing time, an official's bad call, or wins and losses. And sadly, examples of truly egregious behavior, sometimes criminal in nature, are frequent, as PCA's annual "Bottom 10 List" of the worst behavior in sports shows.

PCA's Big Mission

Positive Coaching Alliance has a huge mission: *To transform youth sports so sports can transform youth.* Sports provide an endless procession of teachable moments that can be used by adults to develop great people. But often it just doesn't happen.

That's why we are working hard to promote the Big Picture of youth sports. Our mission will be achieved when the prevailing models in youth and high school sports are:

- **Double-Goal Coaches** who use sports to teach life lessons as they prepare their teams for success on the scoreboard

- **Triple-Impact Competitors** who make themselves, their teammates, and the game better

- **Second-Goal Parents** who concentrate on their children's character development while letting athletes and coaches focus on the first goal of winning on the scoreboard

Just imagine what the experience of sports will be like when coaches, parents, and athletes embrace these roles and play them to the hilt! There is nothing as beautiful as kids and families enjoying youth sports when it's done right.

In Chapter 1 you learned in detail what it means to be a Second-Goal Parent. Now let's take a look at how the Double-Goal Coach and the Triple-Impact Competitor models can make a difference for you and your child.

The Double-Goal Coach

A discussion of the qualities of a great youth coach would require an entire book. But one central idea is critical. Youth sports coaches need to be character educators.

A Double-Goal Coach uses sports to teach life lessons while preparing athletes to succeed on the scoreboard – always on the lookout for the teachable moment in whatever happens on the field, positive or negative.

Double-Goal Coaches work hard to prepare their team to win (first goal), but they never sacrifice the second goal of character development merely to win a game or even a championship. They realize there are few better places to build character than on the playing field.

Youth coaches who measure themselves only by the scoreboard squander that endless procession of teachable moments sports provide. Regrettably, way too many of them do.

There are two ways you can make sure your child has a Double-Goal Coach: get trained and certified as a Double-Goal Coach and volunteer to coach, or look for youth sports organizations whose coaches embrace the tenets of Double-Goal Coaching (and who ideally have been trained by PCA). If your child does not have a Double-Goal Coach, later in the book we'll talk about how you can foster a positive relationship with any well-intentioned coach, regardless of training.

The Triple-Impact Competitor

Your child may not always win, but she can compete well in every game. Teaching your child how to compete well is an important life skill. We developed the concept of the Triple-Impact Competitor for this reason. The traits inherent in this concept – hard work, a teachable spirit, teamwork, leadership, respect – will help your child in sports, but even more in life.

The Triple-Impact Competitor is the highest form of competitor who makes **1)** himself better, **2)** his teammates better, and **3)** the game better.

Triple-Impact Competitors work extremely hard to get better, but they focus on personal mastery and improvement rather than simply trying to win on the scoreboard. (You'll learn more about this in Chapter 5.) They strive to excel and see winning on the scoreboard as a by-product of their march toward mastery.

Triple-Impact Competitors also constantly look for ways to make their team and teammates successful. Where an ego-centered athlete looks for a supporting cast to make him look good, a Triple-Impact Competitor looks to help teammates become better and more productive. This is the essence of leadership and teamwork.

The third level may be the most important for our society. A Triple-Impact Competitor makes the game itself better. He competes hard to win, but by a code of Honoring the Game (which you will learn about in detail in Chapter 7), and would rather lose than win dishonorably.

If you think about it, our current professional sports culture does very little to encourage young athletes to become Triple-Impact Competitors. If a player helps a teammate score a goal, the goal scorer gets the lion's share of the recognition. Linemen who protect the quarterback rarely emerge from the background after a touchdown catch in the end zone. And boorish behavior, showboating, and even criminal activity are tolerated as long as athletes perform well on the field.

Imagine what this world would be like if our high schools were graduating thousands of Triple-Impact Competitors every year. And it can all start with you becoming a Second-Goal Parent.

Chapter 3 Take-Aways

1 Positive Coaching Alliance is committed to changing the culture of youth sports so that Double-Goal Coaches, Triple-Impact Competitors, and Second-Goal Parents are the prevailing models in youth and high school sports.

2 Double-Goal Coaches are character educators first and foremost. They compete to win but never lose sight of the innumerable opportunities sports present to teach life lessons.

3 Triple-Impact Competitors 1) strive for personal mastery and improvement, 2) look for ways to make their team and teammates better, and 3) make the game itself better by competing with honor.

4

Avoiding the Talent Trap

At one time or another, most sports parents will fantasize about their child's success on the playing field – throwing the winning touchdown or swishing the game-winning basket at the buzzer. Some sports parents even wonder, "Could my child have the talent to play in the pros?"

These feelings and aspirations are natural for parents, but here's the reality: the chances of any child – including yours – becoming a professional athlete are not good.

NCAA statistics indicate that fewer than 1 in 200 high school seniors playing baseball will get drafted by a professional team. For football it's 1 in 1,000. For basketball, 1 in 3,333 for boys and 1 in 5,000 for girls. As long as these odds are, they overstate the case because the majority of drafted athletes never make it to the big leagues. Worse, most kids who play sports before high school never play on their high school team.

So concentrating on developing your child's natural talent for a sport in the hopes of helping him become an elite athlete is seldom a winning hand. As we've seen in Chapter 2, there are so many other advantages to participating in sports that have nothing to do with becoming a professional athlete.

But there is a much more important reason to avoid focusing on talent – it can actually harm your child's ability to succeed, in sports and life.

The Growth Mindset

Focusing on talent can be a trap.

Carol Dweck of Stanford University, author of *Mindset: The New Psychology of Success,* has identified two different mindsets that possess enormous implications for sports parents.

The first is the "fixed mindset," in which one sees one's ability as set. Either you are talented athletically or you aren't. Either you are smart or you aren't. This mindset is a dead-end because whether you succeed or not is determined by something totally outside your control.

The other is the "growth mindset." You believe in your ability to grow and improve, regardless of where you start. This is a wonderful thought for any child: "I can get smarter (or better at learning a foreign language or excelling in a sport or...) if I work hard at it."

If your child does something well, either on the playing field or in the classroom, Dweck's research offers clear guidance on how to respond.

For example, you might say, *"Wow, that was a great play. You are really good!"* This focus on talent reinforces a fixed mindset and the idea that the child has little or no control over his development. A tough challenge in the future then becomes even tougher because talented people aren't supposed to be stumped by a challenge.

On the other hand, you could say, *"Wow, that was a great play. You've really been working hard and it's paying off."* This reinforces a growth mindset that her good play is a result of her effort, which will more likely cause her to try harder in the future when faced with a challenge that stymies her initially.

It's All about Effort

Whenever you can, stress to your child how important effort is in helping people improve and learn. Avoid attributing any success your child has to his talent (or intelligence, for that matter) to avoid the talent trap.

You can use "You're-the-Kind-of-Person-Who" statements to reinforce the growth mindset in times of failure and success:

- **Failure:** "I know you must be disappointed (that you missed a key shot, or that you didn't get selected for the lead role in the play), but one of the things I admire about you is that *you're the kind of person who* bounces back and keeps trying until you succeed."

- **Success:** "I was excited to see your improved play. I think you're getting better because *you're the kind of person who* works at something until you improve.

Attributing Your Success

Similarly, you can reinforce a growth mindset with your child when you talk about your own work and accomplishments. I remember times when I solved some problem that had long been vexing me or came up with some idea that I thought was especially clever. I sometimes would say to myself, often in front of my son Gabriel, "I am so smart!"

Now Gabriel is grown and a successful writer with a robust growth mindset, but I realize I would have done better by him if I had said in those times of triumph, "I worked so hard and it paid off in this good idea!"

Developing the Potential of Your Child

A 1985 study led by Benjamin Bloom, *Developing Talent in Young People,* examined children who evidenced talent at an early age in art, music, mathematics, and sport (swimmers and tennis players).

Bloom asserts that there are a lot more potentially talented youth than you might think, as many as 95 percent of all youth. He also concluded that it is hard to identify talent at a young age. Only 10 percent or fewer of the talented athletes could be confidently identified as gifted by the age of 11 or 12. One coach didn't recognize how talented a swimmer was even after working with her for five years.

I think this reinforces Dweck's thesis. Perhaps it's hard to identify talent early on because you always can't tell who is going to work hard over time to develop their ability.

Bloom's study offers some specific "best practices" for sports parents.

Provide encouragement: Bloom concluded that as many as 95 percent of all children have the ability to approximate the achievements of talented youth with proper encouragement. The ones who achieved great things felt a sense of "unconditional commitment." "So far as we can tell, this willingness to give encouragement and support on the part of the parents (and siblings) is one of the major distinctions between the families of these Olympic swimmers and other families." In Chapter 6 we will address how regularly filling a child's "Emotional Tank" can encourage him to achieve his potential.

Model the behavior you want to see: A difference between talented and other children was the example set by the parents who told their children that the sky was the limit: "...the message they passed on to their children was 'you can do anything you set your mind to, if you want to do it...(and) if you work at it.'"

Parents "...encouraged...their children to be disciplined and responsible, and by their own example around the house showed how being disciplined and responsible paid off."

Look for a positive first coach: Enjoyment is important at every step of an athletic career, but it is absolutely essential in the beginning. A positive first coach is crucial.

- "Early coaches were not usually technically expert, but they were great encouragers and enthusiastic about the sport."

- "Perhaps the major quality...was that they made the initial learning very pleasant and rewarding." They gave lots of positive reinforcement, and only rarely were they critical of the child.

- "...they did set standards and expected the child to make progress, although this was largely done with approval and praise."

Manage the transition: Bloom divided the careers of talented young people into three stages, what we'll call the **Romantic,** the **Technical,** and the **Mature** stages.

In the Romantic Stage, the child just loves to play the game. She can't wait to get outside and kick the ball or play catch or jump in the pool.

If the child does well relative to peers, at a certain point, someone – often a parent, but sometimes a recruiting coach – decides the child needs a technically proficient coach, who is brought into the picture to ensure that things are done correctly.

The transition to the Technical Stage is fraught with danger. As the focus moves to technical proficiency, all too often the sport becomes more like a job and less like a wonderful, fun experience. The joy evaporates and the child removes herself from the sports experience as soon as she is able, never reaching the Mature Stage where she is performing at a high level in high school, college, or beyond.

Bloom notes that most kids with talent never make it to the Mature Stage. Why? As we saw earlier, partly because they have lost the joy in playing, which powers the commitment and effort needed to become great.

So it's your primary job to monitor his sports experience to ensure that fun remains part of it through every stage. *No one else is going to have your child's interest at heart the way you do.* Here are some suggestions:

- Ensure your child has a coach who makes sports fun while teaching skills and strategy. Before signing your child up for a team, ask the coach if he has been trained and certified as a Double-Goal Coach who teaches life lessons through sports while preparing to win on the scoreboard.

- Manage your child's transition to the Technical stage. Don't allow peer pressure to cause you to enroll your child in a sports experience too intensive for his age, such as playing one sport year round at a young age or playing so many games his enthusiasm wanes.

- Model what you want to see. Be physically active and share how much you enjoy sweating and working hard. (If you aren't physically active, it's never too late!) Make the same connection with your work. Talk often about the joy of working hard to accomplish something.

10 Years and 10,000 Hours

A study by K. A. Ericsson concluded that it takes an individual 10 years and 10,000 hours of deliberate practice to become an elite athlete. If a youth athlete is not enjoying his sport, he will never stick with it to the point of accumulating the 10,000 hours of deliberate practice time needed to reach the Mature Stage.

The important lesson here is that sports parents need to manage the transition to ensure their child isn't rushed into the Technical Stage. More and more youth athletes at younger and younger ages are playing on year-round travel teams that play so many games that the wonder and joy of playing can be lost.

A child expected to "work" at the sport too soon is more likely to turn off and never reach the Mature Stage. A too-early focus on technique can drain the enjoyment that fuels the drive for excellence.

Chapter 4 Take-Aways

1 Focusing on a child's athletic talent rather than effort is a trap that can actually harm her ability to reach her potential. It's hard to predict who will be successful in sports because you can't always tell who is going to work hard over time to develop their ability.

2 Foster a "growth mindset" in your child, with a focus on effort and improvement. This will help your child recognize that success in sports and other activities depends more on how hard he works than on his talent.

3 As your child ages, make sure to manage the transition from the Romantic Stage (focus on fun) to the Technical Stage (focus on doing it right). Leaving the Romantic Stage too early can make sports feel more like a job and less like a fun experience. Your child must have a love for the game to put in the hard work over time to get really good at it. A positive coach is important at every age, but it is especially important in an athlete's early years.

CHAPTER FIVE

Watering the ELM Tree of Mastery

I remember sitting in a sport psychology lecture nearly 10 years ago trying desperately to make sense of the tables of tiny numbers on the screen behind the speaker. Reminded of an old joke about an optimistic boy surrounded by horse manure, I kept thinking, "There must be a pony in here somewhere."

I took pages of notes but couldn't quite figure out the "so-what factor" for coaches and sports parents. This troubled me because I had just launched Positive Coaching Alliance and I felt obligated to translate the powerful insights of sport psychology into practical tools that millions of coaches and sports parents – the vast majority of whom have no access to a sport psychology consultant – could use to get the best out of athletes.

A few days later while on a long run it hit me. The key principle of sport psychology that was underpinning the complex lecture is that you get the best results when you focus on what you can control and block out the rest.

That's it. That is the secret of sport psychology: focus on what you can control and block out the rest.

Now this is a big idea, with implications far beyond the playing field. But what is controllable and what isn't in the lives of athletes? The biggest uncontrollable is the scoreboard outcome of a competition. You can't control who wins a game: the quality of your opposition, officials' calls, the weather, and injuries all affect the outcome. The list of uncontrollables is endless.

Then what are the crucial aspects of competition that you can control?

That question led to a formulation that has been a central idea of Positive Coaching Alliance ever since, the ELM Tree of Mastery.

The ELM Tree of Mastery

The ELM Tree of Mastery is

E for Effort,
L for Learning and improvement, and
M for Mistakes, how we respond to mistakes and the fear of them.

What was buried in the initially mystifying sport psychology lecture were the three keys to success in sports (and life, for that matter).

Your child absolutely will be successful sooner or later if she

- routinely gives her best effort
- has a "teachable spirit" and learns from everything that happens to her
- doesn't let mistakes (or fear of mistakes) stop her

Redefining "Winner"

Whereas the larger culture is obsessed with results on the scoreboard, the ELM Tree focuses on how hard you work.

Implicit in the ELM Tree is that comparisons with others are not helpful. The person you want to compare yourself to is you. Are you better than you were two weeks ago? Will you be better at the end of the season than you are now? If so, you will be a winner, regardless of the temporary results on the scoreboard.

Emphasizing the ELM Tree of Mastery, and not results on the scoreboard, is what I call redefining "winning." Let's compare the "scoreboard" definition of a winner with the "mastery" definition.

Scoreboard Definition	Mastery Definition
Results	Effort
Comparison with others	Learning and improvement
Mistakes are not okay	Mistakes are okay

The Power (and Paradox) of the ELM Tree

There is a lot of research and supporting material behind the ELM Tree of Mastery, but let me put it simply.

- **ELM = Control:** Athletes can't control the outcome of a competition. But they absolutely can learn to control all elements of the ELM Tree: a) their level of effort, b) whether they learn from their experience, and c) how they respond to the inevitable mistakes they will make. Internalizing the ELM Tree makes athletes feel more in control of their own destiny.

- **Anxiety:** When athletes feel in control, their anxiety decreases. Decreased anxiety frees up nervous energy so it can be focused on accomplishing a task rather than worrying about failing.

- **Self-Confidence:** Self-confidence also increases when athletes feel in control. And when self-confidence increases, athletes tend to work harder and stick to it longer as research by Stanford's Albert Bandura has demonstrated. This is a huge idea, so I am going to repeat it: if you increase a child's self-confidence, he will work harder and stick to a task longer without giving up.

That's the power of the ELM Tree. The paradox is that by focusing on mastery, athletes actually do better on the scoreboard. You win more by not focusing on winning!

Research bears this out. During the 2000 Summer Olympics, sports psychologist Joan Duda of the University of Birmingham, England, conducted research on athletes coached in a mastery environment and those coached in a traditional "scoreboard" environment with a primary emphasis on bottom-line results. She discovered a statistically significant difference in performance – athletes coached to focus on mastery won significantly more medals than their counterparts whose focus was on winning medals.

Athletes will internalize the ELM Tree if they have coaches and parents who emphasize the ELM Tree and de-emphasize results on the scoreboard. This, in turn, helps them feel in control, experience decreased anxiety, and feel more self-confident, so they can perform better.

Here's how you can provide this advantage for your athlete.

The ELM Tree Needs Constant Watering

It is not enough to just tell your child about the ELM Tree of Mastery. The culture of professional sports is not about the ELM Tree. Rather, the dominant sports culture constantly undermines a mastery approach by focusing almost exclusively on scoreboard winners, ignoring great efforts that come up short, showing disdain for those who don't win, and showing and telling in so many ways that the only thing ultimately that matters is winning on the scoreboard.

It is not surprising in light of the 24/7 media saturation in professional sports that it is hard for a mastery approach to youth sports to take hold. That's where you come in.

The ELM Tree requires constant watering. Introduce the ELM Tree to your child and talk about it often.

- **Before a game:** "Have fun at your game today, Emily, and remember the ELM Tree. Give your best effort, look for ways you can learn and improve, and don't get flustered if you make a mistake."

- **After a game:** "I really liked the way you worked the ELM Tree today. You didn't let that mistake in the third quarter keep you from refocusing on the rest of the game!"

The more you use the ELM Tree vocabulary with your child, the more it will help her focus on what is important.

If you as a Second-Goal Parent are able to help your child internalize the ELM Tree, you will have given a wonderful gift that will enhance his enjoyment of sports for years to come. It will also provide him with an approach that will work equally well in the world beyond the playing field.

The Mistake Ritual

No successful person is successful in everything. Many successful people credit their success to being willing to risk making a mistake and learn from it. Chris Larsen, the co-founder of E-Loan and co-founder and CEO of Prosper.com, tells of sitting in Jim Collins' entrepreneurship class at the Stanford Graduate School of Business. Collins, author of *Good to Great,* told the MBA students they were too risk averse. They could afford to fail a few times, learn from their mistakes, and then go on to succeed. The phrase that Chris remembers was, "Cut the lifeboats." Chris says that he likely would never have started a new company like E-Loan if he hadn't heard Collins' comment about the lifeboats and not fearing mistakes.

Mistakes are what kids worry about the most. An athlete on the field feels exposed for all to see. The fear of making a mistake occupies so much mindshare of youth athletes that it can paralyze them. If we can reduce the fear of making a mistake, there will be much more energy available to trying to learn the game and excel at it.

At PCA we've developed the "mistake ritual" as a tool to help athletes learn to not fear mistakes and to bounce back from them quickly.

A mistake ritual is simply a gesture and/or statement that individuals use to ward off the fear of making mistakes so they don't play timidly. A mistake ritual allows you to quickly "reset" and get ready for the next play or decision without wallowing in the past and beating yourself up for having made a mistake.

There are many mistake rituals, but here are two that we especially like. One is "Flushing Mistakes." Mistakes stink. What do we do with stinky stuff? We flush it down the toilet.

When your child makes a mistake on the playing field, you can simply put your hand above your shoulder and make a motion like you are flushing a toilet. You can add commentary to the flush: "It's okay, Omar. Flush it. Next play."

Another mistake ritual is "No Sweat." This involves swiping two fingers across one's forehead like you were flicking sweat from your brow. Do this with your child after a mistake and add, "No sweat. Forget it and have fun!"

Talk with your child about the importance of not being afraid of mistakes, and discuss together what mistake ritual he would like to use. You might even go further and make it a family ritual that involves all members of the family.

Chapter 5 Take-Aways

1 Teach your child the ELM Tree of Mastery to help her be successful in sports and life. The acronym "ELM" reminds her to always give her best effort, to have a "teachable spirit," and to not let mistakes (or fear of mistakes) stop her. Because the dominant sports culture undermines a mastery approach, water the ELM Tree frequently so she internalizes it as her own and is able to apply it to challenges she faces in sports and life.

2 The ELM Tree of Mastery works because it focuses your child on what she can control, which decreases anxiety and improves self-confidence. This, in turn, improves overall performance, whether on the playing field or in any aspect of life.

3 Use a Mistake Ritual to help your child learn to not fear mistakes and to bounce back quickly from them.

CHAPTER SIX

Your Child's Emotional Tank

Have you ever stumbled onto something so basic and powerful that it changes the way you see almost everything?

For years I wondered why I could feel great about a talk I gave on Thursday night and feel terrible about the same talk to a similar group on Saturday morning. Then I read about the "Emotional Tank" in Ross Campbell's wonderful book, *How to Really Love Your Child*. Each of us has an Emotional Tank like the gas tank in a car. If our tank is empty, we can't expect to drive across the country. If our tank is full, we can go a long way.

On Thursday, people in the audience filled my Emotional Tank. They nodded their head when I spoke. They smiled and laughed at my jokes. They asked questions indicating they were engaged with my ideas. Some even thanked me afterwards for an insight they believed might help them be a better coach or parent.

On Saturday morning, no one did anything to fill my Emotional Tank. They scowled, nodded off, talked to each other when I was talking. They drained my Emotional Tank.

No wonder I felt like a gift to the audience on Thursday night and a fraud on Saturday morning. And it all revolved around what was happening to a tank I didn't even know I had.

The Portable Home Team Advantage

Athletes do better when their Emotional Tanks are full. We all could use a "portable home team advantage" in our lives. Unconditional support and genuine praise encourages us and improves performance and attitude.

An athlete with a drained Emotional Tank likely will not perform as well as that same athlete with an overflowing Emotional Tank. That's partly why the home team wins almost 60 percent of the time in college and professional sports.

Kids with full Emotional Tanks are more coachable. They are more open to your suggestions. When Emotional Tanks are full, people tend to be optimistic, deal better with adversity, and are more capable of changing their behavior in response to feedback given them, even by their parents!

When Emotional Tanks are low, people tend to be pessimistic, give up more easily, and become defensive in the face of criticism.

Filling and Draining Your Child's Emotional Tank

The Emotional Tank is a powerful idea, but it is not rocket science. You can fill your child's tank – or anyone's, for that matter – in these ways:

Tank Fillers	Examples
Truthful, specific praise	"Nice effort! You hustled after every loose ball." "A better math score! I noticed you studied hard to prepare for the test."
Express appreciation	"You Honored the Game when you congratulated the other team." "Thanks for taking the initiative to clean up the kitchen without me asking!"
Listening	"What else did you like about the game?" "What was most interesting about the book?"
Nonverbal actions	Smiling, clapping, nodding, thumbs up

Praise can be a tank filler, but it needs to be truthful and specific. It's fine to say, "Good job." But it is so much more powerful to say, "I really appreciated the way you took so much care with this task. Your hard work and attention to detail made this a big success."

Be careful not to heap praise when it isn't warranted. Telling a child he is doing a good job when he is goofing around, for example, is doing a disservice to that child. It also harms your credibility, which can be a big problem over time if your child comes to no longer trust what you praise her about.

Listening is one of the most powerful tank fillers, especially when parents listen to their children. Adopt a tell-me-more-attitude to understand what's going on for your child and to foster healthy dialogue. For detailed guidance on this, read about "Empowering Conversations" on page 57.

While we all need refreshers in tank filling, most of us are pretty natural tank drainers. We often find it easier to see what is wrong and comment on it than to reinforce laudable behavior. Here are common tank drainers:

Tank Drainers	Examples
Criticize and correct	"You could have gotten more loose balls. Be more aggressive like Maria." "That grade isn't good enough. You should have done better."
Sarcasm	"What were you thinking on that play?" "Will you ever clean your room?"
Ignoring	"Not now." "Maybe later."
Nonverbal	Frowning, eye-rolling, heavy sighing

The Magic Ratio

Research has shown that the optimal ratio of tank fillers to criticisms is 5 to 1. Professor John Gottman at the University of Washington calls this the Magic Ratio. I love that name because you really do see some magical things happen as you get close to a 5:1 ratio of positives to criticisms.

In Gottman's work with married couples, he found that couples at the 5:1 level tended to stay married, while at lower ratios divorces were more likely. Research in the classroom also indicates a 5:1 ratio is ideal to stimulate children's learning.

You might consider keeping track of your "plus/minus" ratio for awhile to see what your baseline is. Then work to get it up to the Magic level and enjoy the results. In PCA workshops with coaches, we encourage them to strive for the Magic Ratio to keep athletes' Emotional Tanks filled.

Criticism Transformed

Although criticism tends to drain people's tanks, it is not a bad thing. Criticism can help all of us grow and improve. But the catch is we have to be open to hearing and considering the criticism. And that is where the Emotional Tank transforms criticism into receivable feedback.

Part of being a parent is having hard conversations with our children when they are doing something that is not right or good for them or those around them. And being a consistent tank filler doesn't mean you will never have to have a hard conversation with your child. But it does mean that your child will be more likely to change in response to that hard conversation.

There are some proven ways of making it more likely that your child will hear you and consider your feedback. We call this set of techniques "Kid-Friendly Criticism."

- **Avoid Non-Teachable Moments:** There are some moments when it's harder for people to hear and receive criticism. Right after your child strikes out with the bases loaded is not a good time to discuss the benefits of resiliency. There's just too much emotional turmoil. Wait out non-teachable moments and keep your powder dry for later.

- **Criticize in Private:** It's easier to hear criticism in private than in front of others where it is easy to feel embarrassed and become defensive. Respect your child's need for dignity by talking to her privately.

- **Ask Permission:** Sometimes you can short-circuit defensiveness by "asking permission." "Emily, I noticed something about the way you were dealing with a teammate that concerned me. Are you open to hearing it?" If Emily says yes, she is more likely to consider your comment. If she says no, you create great curiosity in her by saying, "Okay, no problem. Let me know if you change your mind." If you come back with the same question later, she is likely to say yes. Of course, there are situations in which you should not ask permission, like when your child is doing something to dishonor the game or putting her or others in danger.

- **If-Then Statements:** People are more likely to take criticism if they feel in control. If-Then Statements do this. "Clint, I noticed you jogged the last sprints in practice. If you run them all out, you'll have more stamina in the fourth quarter when the game is on the line." Notice you are leaving him in charge of whether he goes all out in the conditioning drills, while enticing him with an outcome he wants.

- **Criticism Sandwich:** By sandwiching your criticism between two positive statements, you make it more likely that it will be heard. This tool works especially well when combined with an If-Then Statement. "I like the way you hustled during the fast break drills. That's great. If you gave that kind of effort during the final sprints at the end of practice, you'll be even better in the fourth quarter with the game on the line. Oh, I also like the way you encouraged the teammates who were guarding you during the one-on-one drills."

Adults' Emotional Tanks

So far I've been focusing on your child, but adults also have Emotional Tanks. I encourage you to be a tank filler for all adults involved in youth sports.

Coaching is actually pretty difficult, especially in a fishbowl with parents watching every move. Regardless of how you think your child's coach is doing, be truthful and specific in filling her Emotional Tank. "I appreciate your commitment to coaching Silvia's team. I can only imagine how much work it is."

This will help later if you have an issue with her coaching. The coach will be more open to your suggestion if you previously have filled her Emotional Tank.

Officiating youth sports is also tough work. Sadly, officials get barraged with tank drainers, so they may appreciate tank fillers more than anyone else. Take time to thank them before or after a game for their hard work. "Thanks for volunteering to ref the game. I've refereed a few games myself, and I know how difficult it is. You did a nice job managing the game and supporting the players."

And you will be a real hit with other parents if you notice good things their children do. "Way to go, Jason! Who's kid is that who made that great play?!"

Sometimes You Have to Fill Your Own Tank

The world is often unforgiving. Your child may one day have to perform in an environment where no one will fill her Emotional Tank. Some people believe that the way to prepare children for "the real world" is to get them used to nasty behavior (e.g., via a nasty, snarly coach) so they will be used to it when they encounter it in the larger world.

I reject this idea. I am convinced that people who grow up having their Emotional Tanks filled on a regular basis are going to be more able to deal effectively with bullies or other tank drainers they cannot avoid (such as an abusive boss). For one thing, they may not be as willing to submit to demeaning behavior as people who have been beaten down by long-term tank-draining behavior. They also are less likely to blame themselves for a supervisor's abusive behavior. They are more likely to say, "My boss is a jerk, but I don't need to let it get to me. I'm going to continue doing my job until I can find a better one."

Chapter 6 Take-Aways

1 An Emotional Tank is like a car's gas tank. People with full Emotional Tanks (from praise, thanks, and non-verbal positives) are more optimistic, better able to deal with adversity, and more open to feedback. When Emotional Tanks are drained (with insensitive criticism, sarcasm, and non-verbal downers), people are more pessimistic, give up more easily, and become defensive in the face of criticism.

2 Strive to reach the Magic Ratio. Research has shown that the optimal ratio of tank fillers to criticisms is 5 to 1. Also, use the Magic Ratio with other adults involved in youth sports, like coaches and officials.

3 Provide constructive criticism to your child using Kid-Friendly Criticism techniques that take into account when and how to deliver criticism so your child can hear it and be more likely to act upon it.

CHAPTER SEVEN

Honoring the Game: Sportsmanship Reconsidered

Each year Positive Coaching Alliance compiles a list of the best and worst sports moments of the year. Not surprisingly, the media usually focuses on the Bottom 10 list and ignores the Top 10 list. Often the perpetrators are sports parents:

- A soccer mom, upset with her daughter's performance, pulled over and left her on the side of the freeway after a tournament.
- A softball dad brought a gun to practice to intimidate his daughter's coach because he wasn't giving his daughter enough playing time.
- A wrestling dad rushed out on the mat to body slam his son's opponent because he believed the other boy was cheating.

While we can tut-tut about the individual behavior of the parents who made the Bottom 10 List, the real problem is one of organizational culture.

A Crucial Mistake

At Positive Coaching Alliance, we define culture as "the way we do things here." The underlying problem is that youth sports has adopted the professional sports way of doing things.

As we discussed in Chapter 3, professional sports is an entertainment business with the goal all businesses have of making a profit. This requires entertaining fans, which in turn usually requires a winning team. Thus at the professional level, a win-at-all-cost mentality too often prevails. And because winning seems so important, pro sports fans tend to see their role as doing whatever they can to help "their" team win.

Because youth sports resembles professional sports – in rules, equipment, strategy – many people make the crucial mistake of thinking the two are the same. But pro sports and youth sports are fundamentally different enterprises. Youth sports is about developing youth into great people who contribute to their society and achieve success in their careers and family lives.

That means that sports parents need to behave in a completely different way from pro sports fans – behavior we call "Honoring the Game."

The ROOTS of Honoring the Game

Honoring the Game is a more robust version of sportsmanship. Unfortunately, sportsmanship has lost much of its power to inspire and now seems like a list of don't-do's, like "Don't yell at officials" or "Don't throw your helmet." Honoring the Game is a concept to inspire and motivate people to live up to their best, rather than simply to be restricted from acting down to their worst.

The ROOTS of Honoring the Game describe the behavior we want to teach and model, where ROOTS represents respect for: **Rules, Opponents, Officials, Teammates,** and **Self.**

Rules: We want to win the way the game is supposed to be played. We refuse to bend the rules even when we can get away with it, whether anyone is looking or not. Rules have been developed and carefully modified to make games as fair as possible. Breaking them undercuts fairness.

No rulebook can cover every situation. There will always be ambiguity that the rules simply don't address. Crafty individuals can find ways to circumvent the exact wording of any rule. People who Honor the Game respect both the spirit and the letter of the rules.

Opponents: A worthy opponent is a gift.

Imagine a tug-of-war with no one at the other end of the rope. Without opponents, competitive sports make no sense. It's not much fun to beat up on a much weaker opponent (or be tromped by a much stronger one). We are challenged when we have a worthy opponent, one who brings out our best. Just think about how the level of play is elevated when evenly matched rivals compete against each other.

"Fierce and friendly" says it all. You try as hard as you can to win. If you knock down an opponent going for the ball, you grab the loose ball and try to score. But when the whistle blows, you help your opponent up. Sports give the chance to get to know athletes you compete against, even become friends with them, without ever letting up when the game is on.

Officials: Officials are integral as guides to fairness in the game. Honoring the Game means you respect officials even when you disagree, even when they are wrong. There is never an excuse for treating officials with disrespect. No matter what.

Teammates: Never do anything, on or off the field, to embarrass your teammates. Honoring the Game involves behaving in a way that one's teammates and family would be proud of.

Self: The foundation of Honoring the Game is respect for oneself. Individuals with self-respect would never dishonor the game because they have their own standards that they want to live up to. Always.

I'm often asked if I expect people to Honor the Game when their opponents don't. That's what having your own standards means. You don't lower your standards because someone else does, even an opponent who gains an advantage. If your child wins by dishonoring the game, of what value is the victory?

Your Role in Honoring the Game

At the heart of the Honoring the Game concept are principles of respect, fairness, integrity, grace, teamwork, and self-respect. These are all values we want to instill in our children, on and off the playing field. Here are concrete actions you can take to help instill these values as you teach your child to Honor the Game.

Model Honoring the Game

Your actions, more than anything else, will teach your child about Honoring the Game. As you share in your child's sports experience:

- Talk about opponents respectfully, and never demonize them as "the enemy."

- Cheer good plays by both teams. One father set the goal for himself that someone who doesn't already know which team his child played on wouldn't be able to tell from his sideline behavior.

- Demonstrate respect for officials by not responding to missed calls.

- Thank and shake hands with the officials after the game. And have your child do so as well. As those of us who have tried it know, officials have the most difficult – and thankless – job in sports. Most youth sports officials are paid little or nothing for their efforts and are subject to abuse from adults on the sidelines. They deserve our gratitude and respect.

Seize Teachable Moments

With ROOTS of Honoring the Game as a framework, youth sports provide an endless procession of teachable moments. Seize those moments to talk with your athlete about them.

- Introduce ROOTS to your child early and refer to it often. Whenever a member of your child's or the opposing team does something that Honors the Game (or not), you can use it as grist for a conversation. "Did you think what that player did was Honoring the Game? Why or why not? Which part of ROOTS was violated or upheld?" Likewise, watching sporting events with your child presents countless opportunities for reinforcing the ROOTS of Honoring the Game.

- The S in ROOTS especially provides many opportunities to encourage athletes to commit themselves to Honoring the Game. You can tell your child, "I don't want you to Honor the Game because it's important to me. I want you to Honor the Game because it's important to you!"

Become a Culture Keeper

Your first responsibility as a sports parent is to model behavior that Honors the Game. But consider going further. PCA has pioneered the idea of a "Culture Keeper" who assists the coach by working with parents on the sideline to keep everyone Honoring the Game. You can do this unofficially by simply encouraging other parents on the sideline to also Honor the Game. If a parent of a player on your team begins to berate the official, you can gently say, "Hey, that's not Honoring the Game. That's not the way we do things here."

Develop a Self-Control Routine

If you are the kind of person who gets upset at games, develop a self-control routine you can use when something happens that might trigger your temper, such as an official making a bad call or an opposing player doing something disrespectful. Imagine things that hit your hot buttons and see yourself remaining calm.

Count backward from 20, turn away from the game to take several deep breaths, or talk to yourself. ("I can do this. I can model respectful behavior for my child.") One mother's self-control routine involved exercise. Rather than watch from the sideline, she walked around the field before the game to ensure there wasn't anything that might trip her up. Then during the game she continuously circled the field. She improved her fitness while keeping up with the game at a distance that left the game in the hands of the players.

Be aware of your tendencies. We've all seen childish or reprehensible behavior in the stands or on the sidelines at youth sports events. Many normal, well-adjusted individuals do things in the heat of their child's games that they are embarrassed about later. Recognize the danger that you, too, may succumb to this temptation, and have a plan for nipping it in the bud.

Chapter 7 Take-Aways

1 Adults in youth sports often make the crucial mistake of adopting the win-at-all-cost mindset of professional sports. Recognize that the real purpose of youth sports is character development, and embrace the idea of Honoring the Game.

2 The ROOTS of Honoring the Game describes the behavior adults should teach and model: respect for Rules, Opponents, Officials, Teammates, and Self. Honoring the Game goes beyond sportsmanship, and sets a standard to inspire and motivate people to compete – win or lose – with class and grace.

3 You can teach your child how to Honor the Game by modeling respectful behavior, seizing teachable moments when participants honor the game (or not), becoming a Culture Keeper, and developing a self-control routine to ensure you remain calm on the sidelines.

8

Test Yourself: Case Studies in Second-Goal Parenting

PCA has more than a decade of experience working directly with sports parents. Through our work with the thousands of sports parents we have served, we've gained an intimate knowledge of the most pressing issues and concerns they have as they strive to support their kids' sports experience.

In this chapter, I share some of the most frequently-asked questions – in the form of short "case studies" – so you can apply the ideas you've learned in this book. In essence, you get to "practice" how you might use a Second-Goal focus in these situations before you encounter them with your child.

The heat of the moment provides a good test. The more you anticipate the kinds of situations you may encounter and think through how you want to act, the more successful you will be as a Second-Goal Parent.

To get the most from these case studies, decide (or even write) what your objective is in each situation and then what action you can take to further that objective. Do this before reading my thoughts. Better yet, talk over the case studies with your spouse or other parents.

Keep in mind that while my thoughts on the case studies are informed by some of the best minds in youth sports, all kids and families are different, so no one size fits all.

Case Study 1: **Your child is about to play in an important game. In the hours leading up to the game, you notice your child seems particularly nervous. As a Second-Goal Parent, what should you do?**

Recognize that nervousness and fear are a part of sports. Particularly as kids get older, knowing that their performance matters can cause anxiety. The objective is to help your child learn to deal with the fear that often accompanies performances – in sports or any activity. This is much more important than how well he performs in this particular situation.

Here's what you can do:

■ Make sure your child knows that he doesn't have to perform well to please you. This may seem silly, but children often get confused about this. "Enrique, I want to make sure you understand that I love you no matter how you perform today. You don't have to do anything to make me proud of you. So go out there and have fun." Then act the part. If he does well, don't go overboard in showing your delight. If he doesn't do well, maintain an even keel about that as well.

■ Acknowledge nervousness and fear directly. Refusing to acknowledge fear of failure doesn't make it go away; it goes underground where it can do real damage. "Just about all great athletes get nervous before a big competition. Remember, nervous is normal." If you have a good story about a time when you were nervous before a game, you might share that story with your child, especially if it has a positive ending.

■ Reinforce the elements of the ELM Tree (Effort, Learning, bouncing back from Mistakes). Because the elements of ELM are more under your child's control than results on the scoreboard, encouraging her to focus on giving her best effort can reduce her anxiety. "Katie, I know you want to win today, but if you give your best effort, you'll be a winner in my book no matter what the outcome."

■ If you (or your child's coach) have introduced a mistake ritual to your child (as discussed in Chapter 5), this is a good time to refer to it. "I hope you remember to use your mistake ritual to flush away any mistakes so you can focus on the next play."

Case Study 2: In a tight game, the official makes a questionable call putting your child's team at a disadvantage. A parent of a player on your team begins to loudly berate the official. As a Second-Goal Parent, what should you do?

There are two objectives worth considering in this situation. A good minimum objective is to make sure that you behave in a way that Honors the Game. A worthy, more ambitious objective would be to help defuse the situation with the verbally abusive parent.

Here's what you can do:

■ Bite your tongue about the official's call. If you have to turn away or even walk away from the sidelines to maintain your composure, then do it. Yelling at officials is the last bastion of seemingly acceptable verbal abuse in our culture, and it is driving youth sports officials away in droves. Whatever you do, make sure that you are not part of this problem. Honor the Game no matter what.

■ You can help calm the abusive parent in a number of ways. It is much easier to do this if your coach has already made Honoring the Game part of the team's culture. If so, use that vocabulary now.

"John, remember Coach told us he wants the team to Honor the Game."

This may provoke a response: "But that was a terrible call! That official is incompetent!"

This is a good thing, as the parent is now talking with you rather than continuing to abuse the official. You can respond again to calm the situation. "It may have been a bad call, but we don't want to do anything that embarrasses our kids. We need to model how to Honor the Game."

■ Whatever you do, don't do anything that will make the situation worse. You don't want to invade the other parent's personal space, nor threaten him in any way. If you don't think you can be a calming influence, it's better to stay out of it.

■ Unless you are in an extremely rare situation where the official is biased against your child's team, calls will go both ways. You can defuse tension by calling attention to good calls that officials make as well as bad calls that go against the other team (which are usually ignored while calls against "our" team are held close and picked over like a scab). "Wow, that seemed like a really bad call. It helped our team, but it was wrong. I guess the bad calls are going both ways today."

■ Make a point of thanking officials after the game. This may be difficult if the official made calls that hurt your child's team and even more challenging if the calls led to a loss, but I bet you can do it.

"I'd just like to thank you for officiating the game today. I know you don't do this for the money, so I wanted to express my appreciation. Thank you." Then enjoy seeing the officials look grateful or amazed (or both)! And feel good about your ability to Honor the Game under trying circumstances.

Case Study 3: **Your child makes a glaring mistake in the middle of the game that leads to an opponent's score. Right afterwards, your child looks over and your eyes meet. As a Second-Goal Parent, what should you do?**

This is a fantastic opportunity to demonstrate your unconditional support of your child while simultaneously reinforcing the M in the ELM Tree of Mastery – learning to handle mistakes without getting thrown off kilter.

Perhaps the biggest fear athletes have is making a mistake in a crucial situation that hurts their team and makes them look stupid. Standing by your child in this embarrassing situation is a most effective way of demonstrating that your love and support for her is unconditional. It may be easy to say you love your child unconditionally – this is a chance to show it.

Here's what you can do:

■ Show that the mistake is no big deal in the grand scheme of things by flashing a thumbs up sign, smiling, or saying, "That's okay, Erica. Don't let it stop you. You'll get the next one."

■ Use a Mistake Ritual if you or the coach has introduced one, like the Flush or No Sweat (as described in Chapter 5).

■ Avoid sending a negative message about the mistake. Don't turn away from your child. Don't grimace, roll your eyes, yell advice ("Never make a cross court pass like that!"), or show that you are upset.

Case Study 4: **You've just finished watching your child's third game of the season, and you already see a problem with the coach. He plays players in the wrong positions and makes bad strategic decisions. As a Second-Goal Parent, what should you do?**

Your main objective in this situation is to retain your Second-Goal focus. You are not the coach. You are not the athlete. You are a supporting player in this drama, so act your part and move to the background.

You might think about the Hippocratic Oath doctors take: Do no harm. Doctors do nothing if they think they might make things worse. The chances of you improving this situation by making strategic suggestions are very small, while the chances of making things worse for your child or for the team are significantly higher. Do no harm. Stay out of this.

Here's what you can do:

■ Write on a piece of paper your strategic suggestions for how you think your child's coach should handle the team. Put it in an envelope. On the outside of the envelope, write "For when I become the coach." Put it in a safe place. Whatever you do, don't give the suggestions to the coach.

■ Let your child have her own experience with this coach without you taking over. Having a coach who makes bad strategic or tactical decisions isn't a tragedy. Most youth coaches are not Phil Jackson or Doc Rivers (and even these amazing coaches get lots of criticism from fans whenever anything they do fails to work perfectly). But that's okay. Your child will have talented and untalented supervisors in his life, and learning to deal with both kinds is a great life lesson.

■ There are a number of reasons to intervene with your child's coach. Among them:

• The coach is verbally or physically abusive to your child or others on the team.

- The coach is draining the enjoyment from your child's love of sports.

- The coach is engaging in unethical behavior.

This is not any of those, so let it be.

■ Thank the coach for his time and effort after each game and each practice, without making any suggestions about his coaching.

Use the guidelines described in the Coach-Parent Partnership, found on page 59, to help your child have the best experience with any coach.

Case Study 5: Your child plays in a league that mandates minimum playing time for each player. Your child consistently plays the minimum amount, and never when the game is on the line. The same players always play more than the minimum and are in at crunch time. You don't think this is fair. As a Second-Goal Parent, what should you do?

The most important objective here would be to help your child have a positive experience this season so he'll be likely to want to continue playing next year.

Here's what you can do:

■ Find out if this is problematic for your child. Although you are frustrated with his amount of playing time, he may not be. And you can do this without asking him. If you ask about whether he is frustrated by the amount of time he is on the field, you may be planting an unhelpful seed in his head.

Instead, watch him. Is he excited to go to practice and games? Does he have a lot to tell you about after games? These are signs that he is engaged and that he is not upset by his playing time.

■ If you come to believe that he is indeed discouraged by not playing more, you can suggest that he approach the coach to see what he can do to get more playing time. Most coaches do not appreciate a parent coming to them to complain about playing time, but I have met few coaches who aren't open to a player asking them about it.

Imagine your child saying something like, "Coach, I'd really like to play more. Do you have any suggestions for things I can do to be able to play more?" This is much more likely to have a good result. The coach may give him exercises to work on outside of practice. He may look for more opportunities to increase his playing time now that he knows the player is hungry to play more.

Perhaps the best thing to come from such a conversation is that your child will have an experience talking with his coach that will be a model for dealing with supervisors and others throughout his life.

Case Study 6: Your child had a chance to make the winning play in the game but missed the last-second shot. The game is over. The team lost. You're in your car driving home. As a Second-Goal Parent, what should you do?

Your main objective in this case would be to reinforce the Big Picture with your child. Taking away something that will help your child later in life – like developing resilience to bounce back after tough losses – is much more important than the result of this particular game (Little Picture).

Here's what you can do:

■ Avoid the dreaded post-game analysis. That's an entirely First-Goal focus (Little Picture) and isn't your job unless your child comes to you and asks for shooting tips. Remember, you have a more important job as a Second-Goal Parent.

■ Don't assume your child is upset more than momentarily by missing the shot. Ask how she feels about the game and then listen carefully before you say anything. Particularly with younger children, they may not even be aware of the "importance" of the missed shot. And even if they are, the missed shot and tough loss may be long forgotten once the post-game snacks are served. Quite often, the adults place greater importance on the outcome than the kids do. If you do sense your child is upset, give her time to process what happened and discuss her feelings at a later time.

■ When you do raise the subject of the game, use open-ended questions to get your child to talk while you stay in listening mode. "What was the best part of the game today?" "What was the hardest part of the game for you?" "What lessons can be learned from a tough loss?"

■ Without downplaying your child's disappointment, lend perspective and fill her Emotional Tank by pointing out things that did go well in the game.

- "You were really in the zone for most of the game today. All your practice is paying off."

- "Both teams competed so hard. I hope you can feel good about your effort."

■ Come back to the Big Picture. "I can imagine it must be disappointing to have lost today's game, but I know you're the kind of person who doesn't let a setback keep you down for long. That kind of resilience will help you rebound from any obstacle life throws your way."

Case Study 7: Your child was very excited at the beginning of the season. Now it seems like every practice he comes home a little more down. You are worried about his morale. As a Second-Goal Parent, what should you do?

Your objective in this situation should be to find out what is draining your child's enthusiasm and enlist his coach in trying to reverse it so your child will want to keep playing sports.

There are two general possibilities here. Either the coach is generally a benign influence or he isn't. In either situation, it would be helpful to see if you can get any insight from your child.

"Gordon, it seems like you aren't as excited about soccer as you were at the beginning of the season. Do you think that is true?" If he agrees, "What about soccer this year makes you not like it as much?" Then listen carefully. If he is willing to share his thoughts on why he isn't enjoying his sport as much, then you can use that in your conversation with the coach. If he doesn't agree, it doesn't necessarily mean that there isn't a problem. It may simply be that, for whatever reason, he isn't willing or able to articulate what the problem is.

Let me now address both coach situations.

Generally Benign Coach: I encourage you to seek out the coach and tell him the situation as you see it. "Gordon seems to have lost a lot of his enthusiasm for soccer. I wonder if you have any thoughts about what we can do to get him excited again?"

If you approach this in a non-blaming manner, it is much more likely that the coach will be open to working with you on this. Even if you believe the coach's style or approach is responsible, you will get further if you don't go into the conversation in an aggressive posture.

Harmful Coach: It may be that your child's coach is the problem. Further, it may be that he isn't open to changing his approach in any way. I still recommend that you approach the coach as above. When it becomes clear that he is not going to be helpful, you have a couple of options. You can go to his supervisor to raise your concern. You will usually get a much more receptive audience here if you have already approached the coach.

Even if you don't ultimately get satisfaction about this coach, by raising your concern you are making it more likely that there will be change in the future. Many administrators are reluctant to take action during a season, but if there are enough complaints, it may result in action after the season. Your effort here may also cause the coach to take stock of himself and become more positive and encouraging with his players.

Finally, if the situation is harmful to your child, you always have the option of taking him out of this situation and finding another one that is more likely to be a positive one.

But what do you do if you aren't able to make changes in your child's sports experience? Encourage your child not to give up on the sport over one bad experience. "Gordon, I know you aren't having as much fun with soccer this year as last. Sometimes things in life don't work out the way we hope they will. I just hope you will hang in there and not give up on the sport. We'll see if we can't find a better situation for you next year."

Case Study 8: Watching a game on television with your child, a player taunts an opponent after making a great play. The taunted player retaliates. As a Second-Goal Parent, what should you do?

Your objective here is to reinforce character traits and life lessons you'd like your child to embrace. Televised sporting events provide a wonderful source of "teachable moments."

There are two ways to handle these conversations. One is for you to assert what you think of the situation. "I think both of the players blew it. Player A made a great play and then acted like a jerk. But Player B would have done better to have ignored Player A's taunt rather than letting it take him out of his game."

This is fine and is necessary sometimes, but an even more effective way would be to ask rather than tell. "What do you think about Player A's behavior after he made that great play?" It is more powerful and lasting when a young person comes to a conclusion himself rather than simply nodding his head along with something his parent or coach said.

Starting the conversation with a question doesn't mean you can't add your thoughts later and even push back if your child says something that you disagree with. "I agree Player B may have been justified in retaliating, but I would have liked to have seen him control himself and Honor the Game. Even if Player A acted like a jerk, Player B could rise above it. I'd certainly like to see you rise above your opponent's behavior if he dishonors the game."

Of course, the other opportunity watching sports together on TV is to point out positive examples of players respecting their teammates, opponents, the officials, and the rules.

Case Study 9: After practice, your child's coach tells you your child has great potential and should specialize, eschewing other sports and training year-round on a club team. The coach says your child can be a standout in high school (and possibly beyond) and will be best served by specializing in this sport. As a Second-Goal Parent, what should you do?

As I speak to parents around the country, I am more often asked about the pressure they feel to have their child specialize in one sport than any other issue. Often the question is asked in a way that suggests parents feel they have no choice but to acquiesce to the pressure, or their child will fall behind. In assessing whether to have your child specialize or not, your objective should be to determine what makes most sense in the long run for your child's athletic and personal development and for your family, since club sports generally are expensive and require substantial time commitments, including travel.

Here are some thoughts about the decision to specialize (or not):

Consider the right age for specialization. Dan Gould of Michigan State's Institute for the Study of Youth Sports says the problem isn't specialization, but premature specialization. Most athletes who attain an elite level specialize, but it is much later than many coaches and parents believe. The research indicates that for most sports, specialization before the age of 12 is not a good idea. And many believe playing multiple sports until 14 or 15 is an even better idea.

Multiple sports help. If your only goal is to shape your child into a great athlete (which I don't recommend), you would have your child play multiple sports. There are many examples of professional athletes who say their success in their ultimately-chosen sport was enhanced by playing other sports until a pretty advanced age. General sports skills such as balance and game sense can be enhanced by playing other sports. And by playing multiple sports until the teenage years, your child will be better able to identify the sport she really loves and can excel in.

Realize coaches' conflict of interest. Relying on the advice of a coach, no matter how successful or skilled he or she may be, is inadequate.

Coaches may have a conflict of interest – building a winning program, operating a profitable business, or a bias toward specialization – that can skew their perceptions.

Beware the dangers of specialization. While year-round focus on a single sport may speed up the acquisition of skills, there are dangers that can outweigh that advantage. Chief among these are burnout and over-use injuries. There are few activities that don't get old when you do them all the time. Year-round specialization makes burnout more likely. Repetitive stress injuries also increase with specialization. Whereas kids playing multiple sports get sore *muscles* at the beginning of the season, athletes who specialize early tend to develop increasingly sore and often damaged *tendons* and *joints* all year long from repetitive use with little rest. The shocking increase in overuse injuries among youth athletes in recent years is a testament to this.

Include your child in the decision. I am much more open to specialization when the child is the one driving the decision. If a child says he wants to focus on a single sport year round, he will be less likely to burn out, for example. Depending on the age of the child, involving him in this decision can be a learning experience. Learning to weigh the pluses and minuses of important decisions is a life lesson. I recommend this even if you ultimately decide against your child's inclination. Hearing him and considering his desires will strengthen your relationship much more than you deciding without his input.

It's up to you. Here's the bottom line: no one can advocate as effectively for your child as you. Resist pressure from coaches and other parents (and perhaps even your child) and make what you think is the best decision for your child and your family. While specialization may make sense for some kids who are passionate about a sport, joining a year-round club team requires a significant financial and time commitment by the family. Some families consider time traveling to and from practice and far-away tournaments as quality family time, while others find it disruptive and onerous. Ultimately you – and only you – are in the position to determine what's right for your child and your family.

9

The Good Old Days

I miss watching my son play sports. When he started playing soccer, basketball, and baseball 25 years ago, it seemed like it would go on forever. But it didn't. It ended abruptly. One day he stopped playing and it was over – just like that and without much warning.

Here's the bottom line for sports parents. Your child's experience with youth sports will come to an end, and it may happen suddenly. If you are at all like me, you will look back and think, "I wish I had enjoyed it more. I wish I hadn't obsessed so much about how well my child was performing, or the team's record, or whether he was playing as much as I wanted, or why the coach didn't play him in the right position. I wish I had just enjoyed the experience more."

If you have a child involved in youth sports, it's not too late for you. Enjoy it while you can. It will end all too soon.

There was a phrase I heard in my youth that has stuck with me: "These are the Good Old Days." Truly, the days when you get to watch your child play sports are golden. If you are still in them, treasure each one of them. Don't let them slip by while you focus on things that will seem totally inconsequential in later years.

Because the youth sports experience is so intense, we tend to forget how short it is, and what a small amount of time that parents and children get to spend together over the course of our lives.

These are the good old days. Enjoy them.

Join the Positive Coaching Alliance Movement

PCA has a huge mission: to transform high school and youth sports into a Development Zone™, where the goal is to develop Better Athletes, Better People and the following become the prevailing models in youth and high school sports:

■ **The Double-Goal Coach®**, who strives to win while also pursuing the more important goal of teaching life lessons through sports

■ **The Second-Goal Parent®**, who concentrates on life lessons, while letting coaches and athletes focus on competing

■ **The Triple-Impact Competitor®**, who strives to impact sport on three levels by improving oneself, teammates and the game as a whole.

If you like what PCA is trying to do, here are some ways you can help:

1) Become a Second-Goal Parent. Use the ideas and tools in this book to help your child have a great experience with sports. You will also serve as a role model for other sports parents to emulate.

2) Spread the Word. Tell people about your experience as a Second-Goal Parent. The more ideas like Honoring the Game, the ELM Tree of Mastery, and the Emotional Tank are discussed, the more people will use them to help their children.

3) Ensure Your Children Have a Double-Goal Coach. Ask if your son's or daughter's coaches have received Double-Goal Coach training. If so, thank them. If not, refer them to PCA's Double-Goal Coach

Online Courses at www.positivecoach.org. You might even invest in those coaches by paying the on-line course fee as a gift.

4) Get Your Schools and Organizations to Partner with PCA. PCA provides a wide range of workshops and/or online courses for coaches, parents, administrators and high school-age athletes. Persuade the leaders of your schools and organizations to visit www.positivecoach.org/our-work, explore our offerings and request more information through pca@positivecoach.org or our toll-free number 1-866-725-0024.

5) Become a "PCA Champion." Promote the PCA Movement through social media:

 Facebook.com/PositiveCoachingAlliance

@PositiveCoachUS

YouTube.com/PositiveCoaching

6) Get the App! PCA's Pocket Sports Quote™ app delivers free daily inspirational quotes from our National Advisory Board Members and others, plus photos that you can swap out with pictures of your own players and share through social media. Find us in the iTunes store!

7) Subscribe to Momentum, Our Free E-Newsletter. Get the latest PCA news, views, videos, tips, tools, information and inspiration for coaches, athletes, parents, and youth sports leaders. To subscribe, visit the "Our Community" section of www.positivecoach.org.

8) Support the PCA Movement. You can make a tax-exempt donation at www.positivecoach.org or by mail at Positive Coaching Alliance, 1001 N. Rengstorff Avenue, Mountain View, CA 94303.

9) Give PCA away. Buy copies of this book for other sports parents you know and check out our books for coaches, athletes and administrators at http://www.balancesportspublishing.com/books

Thank you for helping us turn all of youth and high school sports into a Development Zone for Better Athletes, Better People!

What are YOUR goals for playing sports?

_____ Become a good athlete

_____ Learn to play the sport

_____ Learn teamwork

_____ Win

_____ Gain increased self-confidence

_____ Learn to deal with defeat

_____ Physical fitness

_____ Learn "life lessons"

_____ Have fun

_____ Make friends

_____ Earn a college scholarship

_____ Other (specify: _____)

_____ Other (specify: _____)

_____ Other (specify: _____)

_100_ **TOTAL**

Empowering Conversations

Conversations are the glue between people, the essential element in a strong relationship. Relationships wither without communication, and the very best form of communication is the conversation. Many parents think that it is their job to talk and their child's to listen. Actually that's only half-right. It is also our job to listen and the child's job to talk. It's a wonderful thing when a parent and child can really talk to and hear each other.

Here are some suggestions for how to engage your child in a conversation about sports.

Establish your goal – a conversation among equals: Conversation happen between equals. Kings didn't have conversations with their subjects. They told them what to do. Prepare yourself for a conversation with your child by reminding yourself that sports are her thing, not yours. Remember that you want to support her, to let her know that you are on her side. Your goal is not to give advice on how to become a better athlete. It should be to engage your child in a conversation among equals, one of whom (you!) is on the side of the other (her!).

Adopt a tell-me-more attitude: Keep this thought in mind: "I really want to hear what you have to say." Then listen to what he has to say – even if you don't agree with it – and you will begin to tap into what writer Brenda Ueland calls the "little creative fountain" in your child.

> *If you are very tired, strained…this little fountain is muddied over and covered with a lot of debris…it is when people really listen to us, with quiet fascinated attention, that the little fountain begins to work again, to accelerate in the most surprising way.*

Listen! You may know exactly what your child can do to improve. However, your goal here is to get your child to talk about her sports experience, so ask rather than tell.

Ask open-ended questions: Ask questions that elicit longer, more thoughtful responses. Also ask about life-lesson and character issues.

"What was the most enjoyable part of today's practice/game?"

"What worked well? What didn't turn out so well?"

"What did you learn that can help you in the future?"

Show you are listening. Make it obvious that you are paying attention. Use nonverbal actions such as making eye contact as he talks, nodding your head and making "listening noises" ("uh-huh," "hmmm," "interesting," etc.).

Let your child set the terms: Rather than forcing a conversation right after a competition (when there may be a lot of emotion), wait until your child signals he is ready to talk. Boys may take longer than girls to process an experience, so look for prompts that a child is ready. And conversations don't have to be lengthy to be effective. If he feels like every discussion about sports is going to be long, he may begin to avoid them. Finally, don't be afraid of silence. Stick with it and your child will open up to you.

Connect through activity: Sometimes the best way to spark a conversation is through an activity that your child enjoys. Playing a board game or putting a puzzle together can allow space for a child to volunteer thoughts and feelings about the game and how he performed. This is especially important for boys, who often resist a direct adult-style conversation.

Enjoy: The most important reason why you should listen with a tell-me-more attitude is so your child will want to talk to you. As you both age, you will find there is no greater gift than a child who enjoys conversations with you. Brenda Ueland again:

> *Who are the people, for example, to whom you go for advice? Not to the hard, practical ones who can tell you exactly what to do, but to the listeners; that is, the kindest, least censorious, least bossy people that you know. It is because by pouring out your problem to them, you then know what to do about it yourself.*

Coach/Parent Partnership

The following are some guidelines for how parents can contribute to a Coach/Parent Partnership that can help your child have the best possible sports experience.

Recognize the commitment the coach has made: For whatever reason, you have chosen not to help coach the team. The coach has made a commitment that involves many hours of preparation beyond the hours spent at practices and games. He has earned the right to make decisions (including playing time) with his commitment. Recognize his commitment and the fact that in most cases he is doing so without pay. Try to remember this if something goes awry during the season.

Make early, positive contact with the coach: As soon as you know who your child's coach is going to be, contact her to introduce yourself. To the extent that you can do so, ask if there is any way you can help. By getting to know the coach early and establishing a positive relationship, it will be much easier to talk with her later if a problem arises.

Let the coach coach: You are not one of the coaches, so avoid giving your child instructions during the game. It can be confusing for a child to hear someone other than the coach yelling out instructions during a game.

And remember, the best way you can help your child is to be a "Second-Goal Parent," so focus on helping your child learn life lessons and let the coach coach.

Fill the coach's Emotional Tank: When the coach is doing something you like, let him know about it. Coaching is a difficult job, and most coaches only hear from parents when they want to complain about something. This will help fill the coach's Emotional Tank and contribute to his doing a better job. It also makes it easier to raise problems later when you have shown support for the good things he is doing.

Don't put the player in the middle: Imagine a dinner table conversation in which a child's parents complain in front of her about how poorly her teacher is teaching fractions. How would this impact this student's motivation to work hard to learn fractions? How would it affect her love of mathematics and her relationship with the teacher?

It is all too common for parents to share their disapproval of a coach with their children. This puts a young athlete in a bind. Divided loyalties do not make it easy for a child to do her best. Conversely, when parents support a coach, it is that much easier for the child to put her wholehearted effort into learning to play well.

If you think your child's coach is not handling a situation well, do not tell that to your child. Rather, seek a meeting with the coach in which you can talk with her about it.

Observe "cooling off" period: Wait to talk to the coach about something you are upset about for at least 24 hours after a game. Emotions, both yours and the coach's, are often so high after a contest that it's much more productive if you wait until a day goes by before contacting the coach about a problem. This will also give you time to think about what your goals are and what you want to say.

Note: There are exceptions to the 24-hour cooling off period. If the coach's behavior puts your child's safety at risk, appears unethical, or exemplifies poor sportsmanship, speak to them right away.

When an Intervention is Needed

When you feel an intervention with the coach is needed, the first question to ask yourself is, "Is this something that my child should do for herself?" Consider empowering your child to speak with the coach. If you feel you are the appropriate person to intervene, I recommend talking with your child first, unless she is too young to understand what is going on. If your child does not want you to intervene, you need to decide whether the situation is so bad that you need to do so anyway. As a parent, you always have the ultimate control of any situation in which your child is at risk.